WITHDRAWN

SOUTH CAROLINA

EXPLORE THE UNITED STATES

Sarah Tieck

Big Buddy BOOKS

Explore the United States

VISIT US AT
www.abdopublishing.com

Published by ABDO Publishing Company, PO Box 398166, Minneapolis, MN 55439.

Printed in the United States of America, North Mankato, Minnesota.
052012
092012

 PRINTED ON RECYCLED PAPER

Coordinating Series Editor: Rochelle Baltzer
Contributing Editors: Megan M. Gunderson, Marcia Zappa
Graphic Design: Adam Craven
Cover Photograph: *Shutterstock*: Sydney Beier.
Interior Photographs/Illustrations: *Alamy*: Niday Picture Library (p. 13); *AP Photo*: Cal Sport Media via AP IMAGES (p. 21), Terrence Jennings/PictureGroup via AP IMAGES (p. 25), Marty Lederhandler (p. 25), North Wind Picture Archives via AP Images (p. 23), The Greenville News, Ken Osburn, file (p. 19), Andersen Independent-Mail, Kendra Waycuilis (p. 27); *Getty Images*: Phoenix Photography, Images by Steve Coleman (p. 30); *Glow Images*: Superstock (p. 5); *iStockphoto*: ©iStockphoto.com/jukeboxhero (p. 19), ©iStockphoto.com/Marje (p. 30), ©iStockphoto.com/visionsofmaine (p. 26); *Shutterstock*: Natalia Bratslavsky (p. 27), Dave Allen Photography (p. 17), Gabrielle Hovey (p. 9), iofoto (p. 11), Andrew F. Kazmierski (p. 26), kuch (p. 17), Philip Lange (p. 30), Glenn Price (p. 30), Stacie Stauff Smith Photography (p. 27), JASON TENCH (p. 9), Cary Westfall (p. 29).

All population figures taken from the 2010 US census.

Library of Congress Cataloging-in-Publication Data

Tieck, Sarah, 1976-
 South Carolina / Sarah Tieck.
   p. cm. -- (Explore the United States)
 ISBN 978-1-61783-379-3
 1. South Carolina--Juvenile literature. I. Title.
 F269.3.T44 2013
 975.7--dc23
                                         2012017002

Contents

ONE NATION

The United States is a **diverse** country. It has farmland, cities, coasts, and mountains. Its people come from many different backgrounds. And, its history covers more than 200 years.

Today the country includes 50 states. South Carolina is one of these states. Let's learn more about this state and its story!

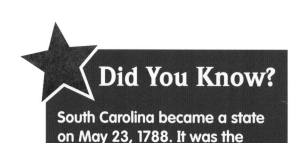

Did You Know?

South Carolina became a state on May 23, 1788. It was the eighth state to join the nation.

South Carolina is known for its gardens.

South Carolina Up Close

The United States has four main **regions**. South Carolina is in the South.

South Carolina has two states on its borders. North Carolina is north and Georgia is southwest. The Atlantic Ocean is southeast.

South Carolina has a total area of 31,114 square miles (80,585 sq km). About 4.6 million people live there.

Did You Know?

Washington DC is the US capital city. Puerto Rico is a US commonwealth. This means it is governed by its own people.

REGIONS OF THE UNITED STATES

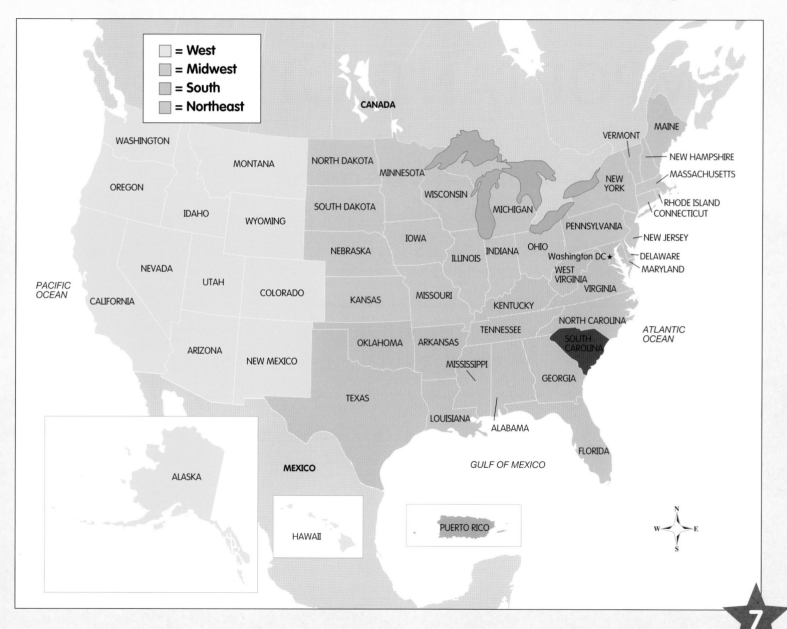

= West
= Midwest
= South
= Northeast

CANADA

WASHINGTON

MONTANA

OREGON

IDAHO

WYOMING

NORTH DAKOTA

MINNESOTA

SOUTH DAKOTA

WISCONSIN

MICHIGAN

VERMONT

MAINE

NEW HAMPSHIRE

MASSACHUSETTS

NEW YORK

RHODE ISLAND

CONNECTICUT

PENNSYLVANIA

NEW JERSEY

NEVADA

UTAH

COLORADO

IOWA

NEBRASKA

KANSAS

MISSOURI

ILLINOIS

INDIANA

OHIO

Washington DC ★

WEST VIRGINIA

VIRGINIA

DELAWARE

MARYLAND

PACIFIC OCEAN

CALIFORNIA

ARIZONA

NEW MEXICO

OKLAHOMA

ARKANSAS

KENTUCKY

TENNESSEE

NORTH CAROLINA

SOUTH CAROLINA

ATLANTIC OCEAN

MISSISSIPPI

GEORGIA

TEXAS

LOUISIANA

ALABAMA

FLORIDA

GULF OF MEXICO

ALASKA

MEXICO

HAWAII

PUERTO RICO

N
W · E
S

7

IMPORTANT CITIES

Columbia is South Carolina's **capital**. It is also the largest city in the state, with 129,272 people. Congaree National Park is nearby. Its forests are known for their tall trees.

South Carolina's State House survived the American Civil War. Bronze stars on the building mark six places where cannonballs hit it.

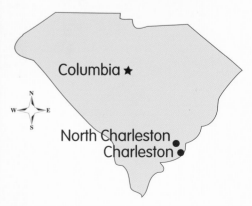

South Carolina

Columbia ★

North Charleston
Charleston ●

N
W E
S

9

SOUTH CAROLINA IN HISTORY

South Carolina's history includes Native Americans, colonists, and wars. Native Americans have lived in what is now South Carolina for thousands of years. The first Europeans arrived in the 1520s. In 1670, the area was settled as an English colony.

Starting in 1775, colonists fought in the **Revolutionary War**. Important battles took place in South Carolina. It became the eighth state in 1788. Later, it fought for the Southern states in the **American Civil War**. In 1861, the war began there at **Fort** Sumter.

On April 12, 1861, Southern soldiers fired the first shots of the American Civil War toward Fort Sumter.

13

Timeline

1775

Colonists began fighting in the **Revolutionary War**. During this time, England's troops were in South Carolina.

1788

South Carolina became the eighth state on May 23.

1865

Northern soldiers burned Columbia during the war.

1700s

1800s

Columbia became the state's **capital**.

1790

South Carolina left the United States to fight for the South in the **American Civil War**.

1860

14

1942

Several dams on the Santee and Cooper Rivers were completed. They supplied power for homes and businesses.

1989

Hurricane Hugo hit parts of South Carolina's coast. Several people died, and many buildings were harmed.

2011

Nikki Haley became South Carolina's first female governor.

1900s

2000s

Insects called boll weevils ruined much of South Carolina's cotton crop. This caused problems for the state.

Senator Strom Thurmond of Edgefield retired at age 100. He is the third longest-serving senator in the United States.

1922

2003

ACROSS THE LAND

South Carolina has forests, sand hills, mountains, and coasts. Beaches lie along the Atlantic Ocean. Major rivers include the Santee and the Pee Dee. The Blue Ridge Mountains are in the northwest.

Many types of animals make their homes in South Carolina. These include rabbits, alligators, and opossums. The state also has more than 300 kinds of birds.

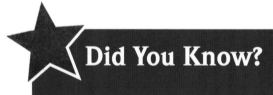

Did You Know?

In July, the average temperature in South Carolina is 80°F (27°C). In January, it is 45°F (7°C).

★★★★★★★★★★★★★★★★★★★★★★★

People often hike in the forests
of Table Rock State Park.

EARNING A LIVING

South Carolina has many important businesses. Some people work for companies that make cars, tires, or plastics. Others work in service jobs, such as for the government.

South Carolina's land provides important products. Its mines provide clay. Its forests provide wood for building. Farmers produce poultry, cattle, hogs, and eggs. They also grow soybeans, cotton, and tobacco.

A famous company called BMW makes cars in Greer.

Many people have jobs helping visitors to South Carolina. Hilton Head Island is one popular vacation spot.

SPORTS PAGE

South Carolina is home to popular college sports teams. The University of South Carolina and Clemson University both have many fans. Their football and basketball teams are often successful.

The University of South Carolina Gamecocks sometimes play the Clemson Tigers. Fans get very excited to watch these rivals play!

HOMETOWN HEROES

Many famous people are from South Carolina. Andrew Jackson was born in the Waxhaw area in 1767. He was the seventh US president. He served from 1829 to 1837.

Jackson was a military leader during the **War of 1812**. Later, he helped create the Democratic Party. Today, this is one of the country's two major political parties.

During the War of 1812, Jackson was so tough he earned the nickname "Old Hickory."

Jesse Jackson was born in Greenville in 1941. He is a **civil rights** leader, **minister**, and speaker.

Jackson is best known for his work in politics. He ran for president twice in the 1980s. He was not elected, but he became known for his speeches.

Over the years, Jackson has founded groups that fight for civil rights. He continues to be active in civil rights and politics today.

Tour Book

Do you want to go to South Carolina? If you visit the state, here are some places to go and things to do!

★ Remember

Visit Fort Sumter in Charleston Harbor. There, you can see where the American Civil War began.

★ See

Walk through one of South Carolina's gardens. Brookgreen Gardens near Georgetown is known for its sculptures.

 ## Play

Spend time at Myrtle Beach on South Carolina's coast. This famous beach is known as a great spot for swimming.

 ## Ride

Visit the Blue Ridge Mountains. You could raft on the Chattooga River or hike in the forests.

 ## Discover

Look up at the tall trees in Congaree National Park. Some are more than 150 feet (46 m) high!

A Great State

The story of South Carolina is important to the United States. The people and places that make up this state offer something special to the country. Together with all the states, South Carolina helps make the United States great.

Hilton Head Island is known for having white sand beaches.

Fast Facts

Date of Statehood:
May 23, 1788

Population (rank):
4,625,364
(24th most-populated state)

Total Area (rank):
31,114 square miles
(40th largest state)

Motto:
"Animis Opibusque Parati"
(Prepared in Mind and
Resources)

Nickname:
Palmetto State

State Capital:
Columbia

Flag:

Flower: Yellow Jessamine

Postal Abbreviation:
SC

Tree: Palmetto

Bird: Carolina Wren

Important Words

American Civil War the war between the Northern and Southern states from 1861 to 1865.
capital a city where government leaders meet.
civil rights the rights of a citizen, such as the right to vote or freedom of speech.
diverse made up of things that are different from each other.
fort a building with strong walls to guard against enemies.
hurricane a tropical storm that forms over seawater with strong winds, rain, thunder, and lightning.
minister a person who leads church worship.
region a large part of a country that is different from other parts.
Revolutionary War a war fought between England and the North American colonies from 1775 to 1783.
War of 1812 a war between the United States and England from 1812 to 1815.

Web Sites

To learn more about South Carolina, visit ABDO Publishing Company online. Web sites about South Carolina are featured on our Book Links page. These links are routinely monitored and updated to provide the most current information available.

www.abdopublishing.com

Index